T0142646

The Love Story of Jesus

By Ashley Henry

WestBow Press books may be ordered through booksellers or by contacting:

WestBow Press
A Division of Thomas Nelson & Zondervan
1663 Liberty Drive
Bloomington, IN 47403
www.westbowpress.com
1 (866) 928-1240

ISBN: 978-1-9736-1776-1 (sc)
ISBN: 978-1-9736-1777-8 (e)

Library of Congress Control Number: 2018901072

Print information available on the last page.

WestBow Press rev. date: 05/09/2018

WESTBOW
PRESS®
A DIVISION OF THOMAS NELSON
& ZONDERVAN

Dedication

To my Love- I dedicate this to my Lord, for giving me the inspiration and all the tools I needed to create this book. God has fulfilled a dream I have had since I was 9 years old, and for that, I am forever grateful.

Acknowledgements

It would take more than a few paragraphs to list all of the people who have supported my artistic endeavors throughout the years. To everyone who has uplifted my art or supported me in any way, shape, or form- you know who you are- and you have my deepest gratitude.

To the teachers who praised and mentored me, the family members who supported me, and the friends who encouraged and shared their time and resources with me, I thank you from the bottom of my heart. Without you, I would not be the person I am today nor would I have had the vision or ability to carry out this project.

To my Mom, Dad, brother, and sister- I want to thank you so much for always believing in my dreams. Thank you for providing for me, encouraging me, challenging me, and pushing me to do my very best. My heart is filled with gratitude and joy at all you have done, given, sacrificed, and invested. I am so blessed to have a family like you. I love you, always.

One day God decided

He wanted to make people

So that He could love them

And they could love Him

He spoke with His mouth

And created bright light

He made Heaven and Earth

And everything in sight

He made water and land

The sky and the sea

Plants and animals

And every creeping thing

He formed the Earth perfectly

Just like He planned

A beautiful home

Built especially for man

And when He had made in it

All that He would

He smiled and said

That all of it was good

God's heart burst with joy

For both Adam and Eve

His eyes sparkled with love

And He was very pleased

Now this He commanded

For all of His people:

"Don't eat from the tree of the

Knowledge of good and evil."

For if they disobeyed

And ate of the fruit

They would surely die

And paradise would they lose

God walked in the garden

With all His creation

Revealing His great love

From morning until day's end

They danced and they laughed

And the Earth they explored

They sang and they danced

And they worshiped their Lord

But one day a snake

Deceived Adam and Eve

They ate from the tree

And so God made them leave

Tears ran down God's cheeks

The day they disobeyed

But He had a great plan

In which all could be saved

He would send His own Son

To live a life free from sin

And then have Him to die

To pay the price of disobedience

Down came His Son

Jesus Christ to the world

Born of both God and Mary

The blessed virgin girl

The Holy Spirit helped

Mary become pregnant

And after He arrived

People brought Him presents

Jesus was perfect

In all of His ways

And often to the Heavenly Father

He prayed

He ate with the sinners

And gave to the poor

He healed all their sick

And did signs and wonders

He taught man how to be

Righteous and pure

Showed them how to love

And worship their Lord

But despite His perfection

In all that He did

Some people hated Jesus

And said, "Crucify Him!"

They beat Him

And put Him on a cross to die

Not realizing that He

Was a sacrifice

Jesus was punished

Unfairly with death

But on the third day

He was resurrected

Then those who had seen

Jesus hurting and cried

Now sang with gladness,

"Jesus Christ is alive!"

And their songs reached to Heaven

To the ears of the Lord

Who beamed with great gladness,

"Relationship is restored!"

For if people believed

Jesus died for their sins

They would be forgiven

And reunite with Him

No longer would God see

Him or her as impure

And He could walk with mankind

As He once did before

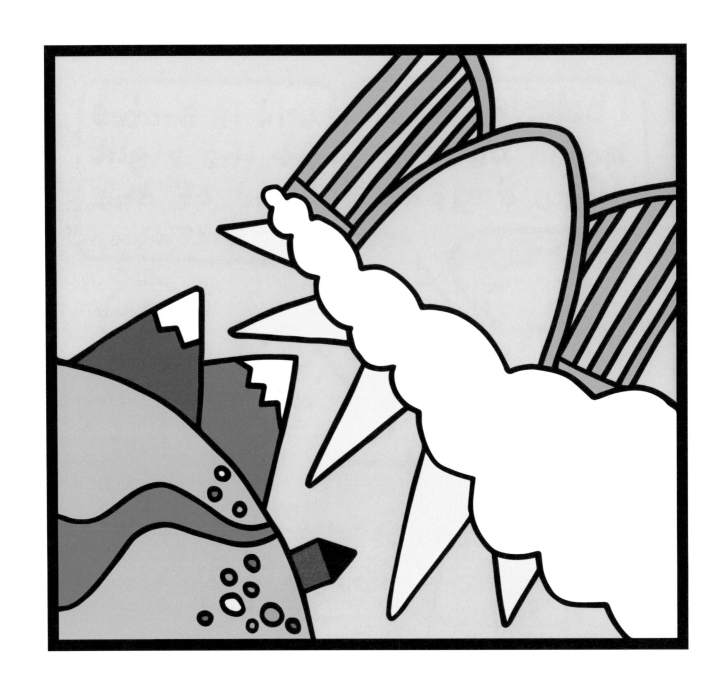

He would show them salvation

And call them His friend

And they would follow Him

From Earth to Heaven

Do you know what will happen

When you meet face to face?

He'll smile and wrap you

In His warm embrace

And He'll show you His kingdom

And Paradise

Where you'll live with Him

For the rest of your life

To jump and to play

And to laugh and to sing

And to love one another

For all eternity

Prayer for Salvation

Jesus paid the price for our disobedience, our sin, so that we could be made pure and have relationship again with Him. He wants to live inside of you, give you the Holy Spirit who will comfort you and teach you how to live a life that is full of love, and connect you with the Father so that you know what it means to be a son or daughter of God. God the Father, God the Son, and God the Holy Spirit are all the same God. They are three in one and He loves you very much. If you believe in what Jesus said and did, you can say a prayer like the one below. God will make His home inside you and be your friend forever.

Prayer

"God, I understand that Jesus lived a perfect life as fully man and fully God and died on the cross to save that which was lost- my identity of love as Your son or daughter. Today, I want to give my life to You and accept You as the Lord and Savior of my life. Thank you for loving me. Amen."

Printed in the United States
By Bookmasters